SURVIVE IN THE OFFICE WITH A SENSE OF HUMOUR

ANDY B

D0608575

www.booksbyboxer.com

Published in the UK by
Books By Boxer, Leeds, LS13 4BS
© Books By Boxer 2014
All Rights Reserved

ISBN: 9781909732216

The Office

So you're an office worker. First of all, let's be clear – working in an office isn't necessarily a bad thing.

You could be doing the job of your dreams in an office – you could be the man responsible for wading through picture after picture of this years 'Miss Slough' entries on your computer (you might want to request your own office with a lockable door if you are) or woman who is Daniel Craig's, very personal, personal assistant.

Whatever it is you do though, working in an office brings with it a whole host of deadlines, dramas and downright baffling dilemmas.

Also, working in an office embroils you in a sociopolitical system that makes general elections look like a walk in the park. So how do you deal with all this without throwing your computer at the wall, putting your tie through the shredder and walking out naked as the day you were born screaming 'I want to break Free!' by Queen? Well, that's when this book becomes an invaluable tool to help you through the tough times.

Yes, if there's one urgent piece of paper work for you to read today, one thing on your To Do list that you shouldn't 'accidentally' erase, one book that's used for more than just wafting farts across the office towards a colleague, it's this book.

From learning how to battle boredom to surviving those awkward water cooler conversations with the person to whom you emailed 'I really fancy you' in error – we've got it covered. So loosen your tie or blouse, kick off your loafers or heels, and get ready for an office training exercise that doesn't involve catching a colleague four times your size, standing up and telling everyone what animal you would be if you had to be one or watching just enough of a clip from Faulty Towers to make you want to watch more, only to have the lights flicked on and a 'super fun' questionnaire slapped in your face.

Just one thing though - read it quickly. There's no overtime available this week thanks to the incident with the photocopier after hours last Tuesday.

You know what we're talking about!

'It is easier to appear worthy of a position one does not hold, than of the office which one fills.'

Francois de La Rochefoucauld

The Anticipation

You filled out a really long application form that asked you like, loads of questions and stuff and made you look up the meaning of the word diligent. You dragged yourself away from 'Homes Under the Hammer' twice, for both a first and a second interview (which were basically just the same, only you felt obliged to wear different clothes on each occasion). You waited by the phone for at least twenty minutes after your second interview for them to put you out of your misery before giving in and ordering a pizza.

Then, finally, after weeks of messing about, you get offered the job and what's more, you get your start date. And guess what - it's this Monday.

'Work is the curse of the drinking classes.'

Oscar Wilde

Now, we know that you're cool, you must have been to get through the application process but after your 8th drink down the local pub, the night before your new career kicks off, you start to feel that jingle jangle, that silly little squirmy feeling in your belly and - after you've been for a wee - you realise that what you're actually feeling is nerves.

And you start to think ... *I never felt nervous in my old job. I knew what I was doing there – it was easy.*

Why the hell did I leave? Why am I put myself through all this?

Your friends try to reassure you that it's normal to think like this but it doesn't stop, the questions just keep on coming...

What will the office be like?

Will it have plants?
I like plants. I need plants!

Will there be a hot receptionist/doorman?

(He) Is my dad's old suit really suitable?
Flares are still cool — right?

(She) Should I buy a whole new outfit?

What if I end up sat next to 'the annoying one'?

What if I'm 'the annoying one'?

What if everybody hates me?

What if I hate everybody else?

What if everybody else hates everybody else?

What if they don't have a vending machine?

What if they do have a vending machine and there's not enough time to go get a tea or coffee and I nearly die of thirst.

What if they do have a vending machine but it's one where there's not enough room between the snacks and the glass so my crisps keep getting stuck and it steals all of my money and I end up homeless and destitute - all because of this stupid office job?!

And then, just as you start to rationalise things and calm down - you start to feel a little funny...

Oh no, what if I can't hold down the kebab I'm eating right now as I'm walking home from the pub...

and then...

blurghhhhh!

And the only question left running around your mind as your dizzy little head hits the pillow is "*What if the owner of the classic convertible I threw up in on the way home saw me do it?*"

Your First Day
New Kid on the Office Block

"Hey, I'm the New Boy!"

How's the reception in here?

Amongst the hustle and bustle of people dragging their feet through reception as their bodies attempt one last futile cling to the weekend, you duck and dive your way to the front desk. And as the receptionist glowers at you through her 4 inch thick lenses, you (in an attempt to lessen attention and/or embarrassment) whisper your name and the fact that it's your first day. After a short pause and a sigh so heavy you could make a good guess at what she had for dinner the day before, you realise just what you're dealing with.

She's grumpy, hard of hearing, too long in service for her liking and chooses to channel the bitterness of her delayed retirement through a means of spite and sarcasm - 'Want to speak up, love? Or are you just gonna stand there whispering sweet nothings at me all day – coz I've got all day haven't I – I've got nothing to do here!' Thankfully for Miss Donkey Breath, you were brought up not to cheek your elders so with a deep breath (which you immediately regret) you do as she says and project the words 'It's my first day' nice and loud - just as everything else around you falls quiet.

One - nil to the reception witch!

Induction

The Name Game

Many companies have different takes on the whole induction thing but someone (usually in an attempt to lengthen their involvement and thus spend longer away from their own desk) will invariably decide to walk you around the whole building and introduce you to absolutely everyone – even people using the toilets (handshakes are not advisable in these circumstances).

So the first question you ask yourself is 'How the hell am I going to remember all these names?'

The answer is; you won't. Therefore, the solution to this particular dilemma is not to even bother trying. UNLESS … you're introduced to somebody really attractive. In these circumstances, it can be worth remembering their name so feel free to try but, if we're honest, the odds are against you and knowing, your luck, you'll probably get him/her mixed up with the employee who has a reputation for being the one most active under the mistletoe at the office Christmas party.

Beware of this type, especially if you are in the vicinity of the stationery room.

Smile!

These days, security is a real issue. So much so that here at Book Writing Headquarters, all the doors have retinal scanners which are so efficient that following a particularly bad case of conjunctivitis, poor old Pete once got himself stuck in the stock room for a month. Naturally, the first thing we said when we found him was, 'You could at least have tidied the place up a bit'.

Now, in your office, security measures will probably stretch to a pass that you swipe across little black scanners on the doors. Feels a bit like, "Men In Black", at first but it soon wears off and it's certainly no excuse for wearing sunglasses indoors.

Now, as well as carrying the annoying element of being easy to forget when you're in a rush in a morning, these passes also carry another dreaded component for all of us camera shy colleagues. Yes, it's the much feared photograph. Now, in theory, this should take place on your first day and your first day is usually the best you'll ever look during any term of employment. This is because every day that follows becomes another test of the 'smart casual' dress code boundaries – a test that ultimately reaches the point where you actually consider wearing the Bermuda shorts your Aunty and Uncle (who always had much fancier holidays than your family) brought you back from their trip abroad a couple of decades ago.

Unfortunately though, they don't always take your photo on your first day.

Life being life, they will often spring this on you the morning after an all-nighter and you leave the photo shoot with a permanent reminder hung around your neck of the day you accidentally wore your girlfriend's blouse and styled your hair with Pedigree Chum™.

Always wear goggles!

During your induction, you're likely to spend an hour of your life being reminded that calculators aren't edible and it's not advisable to build ladders out of staples and blue tack. We are, of course, referring to everyone's favourite reason for getting out of doing anything that involves lifting one light object from one place to another – health and safety.

Now, we do actually take health and safety very seriously here and as such, we're going to take this opportunity to test your current grasp on this most important component of any induction worth its salt.

(H&S note: salt is not very healthy – but can be quite good for you when applied to icy ground you may have to walk over).

QUESTION:

You are walking across the office and notice that somebody has left a bear trap in the middle of the walkway with a packet of your favourite crisps resting in the middle. What do you do?

Do you:

A. Inform your Health and Safety Representative.

B. Edge your way around it, return to your desk and assume that somebody else will attend to it.

C. Call the A-Team.

The answer is – none of the above!

Remember – there's a packet of your favourite crisps at stake here. Now we're not, of course, suggesting you brave the trap to retrieve them – that would be foolish and downright dangerous.

The real answer is -

get a temp to do it!

Mark Your Territory

As much as doing the 'dog and the lamppost' against your desk would definitely stop people stealing your stapler – this is not to be recommended.

Many offices consist of tens or even hundreds of similar little desks and if you're not careful, it can start to feel a little bit like a paper pushing, keyboard clacking version of battery hen-ism.

Therefore, a certain amount of creative individualism may be required to carve your tree.
So, feel free to decorate your desk and those felt covered, plastic, little walls (designed to make you forget you're

part of the human race) with a collection of the little things that help to make you the funny, quirky little person you are.

But remember, your space can tell people a lot about you!

'I was going to have cosmetic surgery until I noticed that the doctor's office was full of portraits by Picasso.'
Rita Rudner

Of course, there's a line and with some things, it's not always easy to determine. Putting up pictures of pets is an example. Now, a picture of Fluffy the cat sat in her basket looking cute is all well and good but having a picture of your parakeet playing Maria in your family's stomach turning, cringe worthy production of The Sound of Music is a little too much.

Also – dogs licking their bits is something no one wants to see.

It's also wise not to display anything defamatory and/or non PC.

And just in case, like us, you're finding it more and more difficult to keep up with the ever increasing list of banned subjects on the PC guide to giggling, here's what we imagine to be the most recent statement:

The world is strictly prohibited from partaking in laughter as a result of any representation of any person or animal whatsoever and, following an amendment to section 35a(i) - those plants deemed to be the most sensitive – including Dandelions (especially when they get all white and floaty and stuff) and any flower whose head hangs down like somebody who looks a bit upset.

So, anything that falls outside of the above guidelines is absolutely fine!

Up and Running
(and screaming and pulling your hair out!)

So, you've met everyone, you've got your pass, you've been cleared as being both healthy and safe and you've got your desk looking just the way you want it. You have, my friend, been thoroughly inducted. This means that you're well and truly ready to embark on an adventure in a world that knows no bounds (well, there's like walls and stuff), a trip that knows no time (well, it's kind of 9 to 5 to be honest) and an experience that words can't describe (until you go for another job then you sort of use words to describe it on your CV).

Yes, you're ready for the leg slapping, labour of love that is...

...life in an office!

'Work is a necessary evil to be avoided.'
Mark Twain

'Hard work spotlights the character of people:
some turn up their sleeves, some turn
up their noses, and some don't turn up at all.'
Sam Ewing

'Not once in six years did I make it to the office by 9 on the dot.'
Joseph Barbera

When asked, "what time do they start work at your place", **Jimmy Goldman** *stated that he didn't know as he'd never arrived at the time work started.*

On Probation!

Yes, it is fairly customary for most employers to insist on a probationary period when you first start a job. This basically means a period of time during which the company can drop you like a hot potato if you really mess up. It also means that at the end of the period, they will review your performance to judge whether or not they want to maintain your employment.

So, on top of everything else you need to remember, here are some other little pointers to help you avoid an early bath during your probationary period:

Don't call your boss 'Mum'.

Don't drop your food tray in the canteen.

Don't fall over or you will be the victim of the chant 'She fell over', (regardless of your gender).

Don't take fish sandwiches. This can be especially hazardous if people can smell it but don't realise it's coming from your sandwiches.

Don't split your pants playing football at break time (especially if you're a girl!).

Don't hand out copies of the controversial screen play you've been working on entitled 'The Fantasies of an Office Worker'

Don't fart at your desk. In time, you will learn how to make clandestine deposits of flatulence but it is too risky during the probation period.

Don't stand in dog pooh on the way to the office. There's nothing worse than being asked the question, 'Is it you that smells of pooh?'

Don't pretend you have X-Ray vision.

Don't block the disabled toilet. Remember it is unisex and you never know who might follow.

Don't take your pet weasel to work, regardless of how badly he suffers from separation anxiety.

Don't sleep with the boss's spouse.

Don't sleep with the boss, (at least, not on the first day)

Don't ask who the office bike is.

Don't become the office bike.

Don't ask for a full body medical from the first aider.

Don't type 'BOOBIES' on your calculator.

Don't type 'BOOBLESS' on your calculator.

Think of something non 'BOOB' related to type on your calculator.

Don't steal office supplies.

Don't slap anyone in the face with a glove in order to challenge them to a duel.

Don't try to be the 'printer whisperer' – those things wouldn't even work for Robert Redford.

Don't tell any sexist jokes – the women probably won't understand them.

Don't tell everyone you're 5th in line for the throne, only to later explain that you meant 4 people were ahead of you in the queue for the toilet.

Don't try and multi-task – it doesn't exist. You can do one thing well, or three things badly. Unless you're a woman.

Don't do your impression of a polar bear and later try to defend yourself by saying 'Since when have you ever seen a polar bear wearing clothes?'

Don't stick photos of your eyes to your glasses so you can sleep sat up at your desk.

Don't perform your Eurovision Song Contest entry.

Don't show everyone your holiday photographs – 'Here's one of the wife stood near a Parrot and here's one of me stood near the Parrot. Here's one of the wife pointing at the sea and here's one of me pointing at the sea. Here's one of the wife kissing the waiter... here, wait a minute!'

Don't act out your favourite scene from Grease. Trust that people will believe you when you say you can sing. And definitely don't wear leather pants. They will seriously chafe.

Getting a Round In!

Now you're settling in to your new life in an office – you've noticed that a lot of people are walking around with trays of drinks. I'm afraid these are not the 'waiting staff' – they are simply your colleagues. Yes, it is an office tradition for each member of a team to take their turn doing a tea and coffee run. Now, this may seem like a good idea but wait until you're on a team of 20 and each person has their own mug, some of which have to be cleaned out before each refill. It's at times like these that you also realise just how many different variations of coffee there are – black, black with sugar, white, white with sugar, latte, skinny latte, espresso, de-caff, etc etc - and let's not even get started on all of those fancy teas. Now, many people may let this overwhelm them and when they get to the kitchen with 20 mugs, 20 different orders and half an hour of washing up to do – they throw the sink out of the window and lollop to freedom.

However, all you have to do is make a list or, if you have it in you, you can develop a little rhyme to help you remember what everyone wants.

Karen's the one who eats toffee,

So likes lots of sugar in her coffee,

But Stace is straight laced and watches her weight

So swerves any coffee that's frothy.

Now Matt's a bit hyper and daft,

So the team make him stick to de-caff,

But Dan, you understand, who's a typical Man -
Gets as much in a mug as he can,

Now I've got one for each of my mates,

But wait – there's that quiet girl Faye,

But I can't hear what she says, so whenever I ask – I just fill up her flask with Earl Grey!

The only place success comes before work is in the dictionary.'

Vince Lombardi

'Work fascinates me. I could sit and watch it all day'.

Tommy Trinder

'There are only two classes: working class and idle class. If a middle class were to exist it would be half working and half idle'.
Lawrence Johnstone

'Faced with the prospect of a lifetimes paid idleness, a man can turn his hand to anything.'
Lord Barkstone of Winterburn

'The brain is a wonderful organ; it starts working the moment you get up in the morning and does not stop until you get into the office.'
Robert Frost

'Loyalty, teamwork, efficiency, - we don't have any of that bullsh*t around here'
Office Sign

'The best preparation for good work tomorrow is to do good work today.'
Elbert Hubbard

Deadline Schmeadline!

There's nothing more daunting in an office job than that 8 letter word that, when uttered, gets folk freakishly frightened, people proper panicked and has been known to cause more late nights and pounding headaches than a Black Sabbath tour – yes, it's the dreaded

D-E-A-D-L-I-N-E !

And there are usually two types. There's the, *'Peterson – can you have this done for me in the next month'* and the, *'Peterson, I need this today!'*

Now, the former is ostensibly the least stressful – Peterson's boss has given him a lot of time, thus enabling him to plan things properly and execute to a high standard. The second one however, means that Peterson not only needs to get cracking straightaway, but is also likely to need some new under-crackers, owing to the shock element.

However, it is very common, very common indeed - in fact, it is possibly something innate to most human beings – that when we are given lots of time, we procrastinate and procrastinate and end up leaving everything to the last minute and find ourselves in a mad rush. Now this is panic of our own making and therefore, not only do we have the stress of doing a month's work in an afternoon – we also like to constantly berate ourselves whilst doing it by saying things like, 'Why I have I done this?', 'What's wrong with me?', 'I'm an idiot!', 'That new starter's pretty fit!'

(Let's face it; no matter how stressed you are – you always notice a new fittie!)

So, whichever deadline drama you find yourself cast in, you need to be prepared for the fact that now and then, you might not meet a deadline. Now, with the word 'deadline' having the word 'dead' within it – this can feel like a somewhat fatal mistake. This will often leave you thinking that you need a good reason for failing; that you need an explanation; that you need a rationale – that you need a blooming good excuse!

However, peddling the same old rubbish about family emergencies and getting your head stuck in some railings isn't going to cut it as your boss may not actually be the blithering idiot you assume she or he to be. Therefore, you need something that is more than just an excuse – you need a well-constructed, thought out admission of failure, followed by an assertive plan of action and a conclusion that explains how this particular error has taught you many lessons that you can take forward to ensure this never, ever happens again.

For example:

'Firstly, let me start by taking this opportunity to thank you for your time. I know it is precious and could be better spent elsewhere at this moment. Secondly, I must sincerely apologise for the fact that I have, on this occasion, not met the requirements of the project assigned to me within the specified time expectations.

I would like to assert that this is the first time I have failed in this regard and as such, would proffer that this failure hurts me as much, if not more than it does yourself and this fine company. I set myself extremely high parameters of performance so in this respect; I have let myself down as much as any other party.

I will not patronise you with a list of reasons—come-excuses but will instead assure you that I am implementing the plan of action that I have forwarded to you by email and this plan determines that I shall complete this project by [INSERT DATE] and I will naturally be working unpaid overtime to achieve this.

Now, before I return to my desk and assume the afore mentioned plan of action – I would like to take a moment to assure you that this experience, whilst being one that I have not enjoyed, has taught me many lessons that I will most certainly carry forward into all of my future endeavours as a member of your team. I can guarantee that this failure will never occur again.

Naturally, this presentation is only good for one failure. Mess up again and you might be back to pretending you got your head stuck in the railings. Good luck with that one!

Employee of the Month
(Swot)

When you do manage to hit a few deadlines and turn a few heads at the powerful end of the organisation, you may find that your performance is recognised and rewarded. Not with a pay rise, oh, no, no, no – something much more valuable than money - something that puts pride in your performance and a certificate on your wall, yes, it's...***Employee of the Month.***

Now, we're not mocking this prestigious award but feel obliged to warn you about the possible ramifications of wearing your 'Employee of the Month' medallion to the canteen, holding seminars for colleagues to learn how to be just like you and generally indulging in the many honours that await each month's victor.

All Work and No Play...

Now, as much as life in an office can at times seem to revolve around burgeoning 'In Trays' and looming deadlines – there are also times when things get a bit quiet ... as well as times when you just fancy a good skive.

"As Employee of the Month you get to be first on the elevator."

But often, you don't really know what to do and therefore resort to one of the following, age old aids to idleness:

Making a necklace and/or matching bracelet out of paper clips.

Making a rubber band ball.

Making a paper aeroplane - only to be disciplined for accidentally throwing it in the eye of Julie from Accounts.

Randomly stapling things together, making something artistic and then spending the rest of the afternoon trying to find the bits of paper as they turned out to be really important memos.

Massive fun!

However, the works of delicate intricacy of these particular time wasting attempts often need to be hidden when that anal guy, the one in charge of the stationery cupboard, (you know - the one who makes you fill in a form and whom you have to address by the title, 'Super Intendant of Stationery', before he'll hand you a pack of

Post-It's™) issues a warrant for missing paper clips and rubber bands and after days of people ignoring him, concedes to an amnesty and leaves a box in a quiet place for people to secretly return things.

The modern office, however, has something that offers more than bits of stationery can ever deliver, something that literally puts the world at your fingertips – it has internet access.

Now, each employer will have a different code of conduct in place when it comes to internet usage during working hours so it's always best to check this before embarking on any online adventures. So, once you know that you're not allowed to use the internet for personal reasons and dutifully decide to ignore this – there are many options available to you. You can read the news, check out your favourite car or fashion website or keep track of the cricket scores.

Whatever you do though, it's always best to use a website you think you can trust. The internet may be a fun place to be for most of us but there really are some strange old things out there, things that could well and truly damage your computer and thus, your wallet (when you're sent packing for accidentally wiping the company's mainframe, because you hooked up to a dodgy site such as **_www.howtoloseyourjob.r.u.an.idiot.nob_**

So our thoughts on this is that internet usage is risky – meaning you'll have to make your own decision on this one.

Then, of course, there is email. Now, again, most companies monitor email use, not only to detect anything untoward being distributed but to also check that, instead of balancing your spread sheets, you're not spending all of your time electronically chatting to your mates or that bird/hunk on the top floor. So again, using email as a means to alleviate boredom comes with risks and is therefore a judgement call on your behalf.

Back to Basics...

Remember the white sheets that everybody used to do work on using blue or black stuff ... hmmm, what were they called – oh, that's it – paper and pen!

Now, these are materials that every office should have plenty of and if you use a bit of imagination, you could quite happily while away a few hours. Here are some ideas/age old things we've all forgotten about that merely need a bit of imagination and/or a pen and paper:

Hangman

Despite the game carrying slightly disturbing connotations of capital punishment – it's great fun! You can find the rules online.

The thing to stress here is that, if you want to win, you need to be really obscure.

For example, the category you and your friend/ competitor have decided upon could be, 'Things you might do at the seaside'.

So whilst everyone else goes for more ordinary things like, *'build sand castles'* and *'paddle in the sea', you might decide to choose – 'draw out all of my money, have it converted into copper and spend it all in the 2p drop machines where the shelves move and if you get it right, small, cheap and not worth much more than 2p prizes fall into the tray – along with some 2p's'.*

Follow this example and whilst you're likely to never get another game of this with that particular person - you're sure to win!

Trivia Questions
(with a strict internet ban)

For example; 'Name a club in the football leagues that has a name whose letters host no complete circles/enclosed areas that could be coloured in (letters such as a b,d,e etc). Tough, isn't it? The answer to this will be provided somewhere in the remainder of this book. Annoying, eh?

Pictionary type game

Yes, you don't need to buy the board game to play this festive favourite. Just split into two teams and when it's one team's turn to draw – the opposing team decides

what the 'drawer' has to illustrate for his team mate(s).
It's a good idea to decide on a maximum number of
words per drawing, not least to prevent that person who
is always banging on about how they should have been a
writer handing over a badly formed sonnet about jaded
love for the 'drawer' to interpret.

The Unfolding Story

This is that game where you start with a blank sheet
of paper and the first person starts a sentence at the
top, then folds it over so it can't be seen and passes
it on. The next person then writes another section of
a sentence and again, folds it over so it can't be seen
by the next person. If you have enough people playing
to fill a whole sheet, unfolding it and reading all of
the sentences one after the other at the end can, on
occasion, be responsible for a slight titter of laughter.
(Not guaranteed).

Doodling

This may often be written off as the meaningless
wandering of the pen holding hand of a bored worker

but, if you actually put some effort in, you can really get into it. Who knows – today's doodle could be tomorrow's priceless art!

Table Football Using Coins

Now, there are a couple of variations to this game and the one we're suggesting is the one where two people sit opposite each other at a table. There are 3 coins involved (usually 5 pence coins) and when it's your turn to shoot, you place the coins in a triangle – making sure the single coin is facing you - then, using the outside of the middle part of your bent index finger, you push/strike the single coin, thus causing the coins to break open. Now, the only way to make progress across the table is to strike a single coin between two other coins

When you think you are in a position to shoot (the goal being provided by your opponents hand on the edge of the table by a means of putting a fist against the edge and then placing only the index and little fingers flat on the table), the coin you shoot with must also pass through two other coins on its route to goal. The turn passes to the other player after a goal, if an attempted shot goes out of play (off the table) or if at any point, the coin being struck does not go between the other two coins. Also, all moves must be of a forward nature. Who needs the Premier League, eh?

Noughts and Crosses

Good for about 5 minutes or so. Not really much else to say about this except you can jazz it up by replacing the noughts and crosses with other symbols. Be prepared for a very awkward conversation however if you're caught playing the game using symbols relating to genitalia.

Rock, Paper, Scissors

Ok, ok - so we're clutching at straws here but if you're of the science fiction persuasion, a version including a lizard and a Spock or something has been devised and the rules can be found online. Live long and prosper.

Am I an idiot?

This is the game where you get a famous name on a piece of paper stuck to your forehead that everyone but you can see and you have to ask questions to ascertain who it is. Not the most subtle of games to play in the office and trying to explain why having the name 'Genghis Khan' stuck to your forehead relates to your job can be a wee bit difficult if you get caught.

And finally –

That Girly Fate Thing

The thing that girls in the playground used to do, where they would conduct some magical origami type folding and end up with four triangles spread across four fingers. Each side to the triangles would have a different word on it. The girl would then proceed to ask you a question and these words would be the multiple choice answers and after some weird hand shuffle thing, they would ask you another question and this would go on and on until they finally unfolded something which revealed that when you grew up – you were going to marry a smelly dentist who drove a Lada.

I suppose, if you're really, really bored!

'I originally welcomed the mobile phone, as it seemed to me that it would enable you to work from anywhere. On the mobile, who was to know if you were sitting on the branch of a tree or sitting in an office? But it instead had the opposite effect: instead of freeing us from the office, it allowed the office to take away our freedom.'

Tom Hodgkinson

'Acting in a stage play is like working the evening shift in an office.'

Arthur Smith

Working in an office with an array of electronic devices is like trying to get something done at home with half a dozen small children around. The calls for attention are constant.'

Marilyn vos Savant

Gone are the days of the humble paper and pen, of the pencil and ruler and lever arch files. Nowadays of course, everything is done on man's faithful companion – no, it's not the dog – it's the computer. And let's face it, computers make a lot of things quicker. For example – today's office worker dissolves into a fit of rage, on average, one million times faster than the office workers of pre- computerisation. Computers also make a massive contribution to production levels with employees now having an array of time wasting options available that the humble pen and paper struggle to provide. Plus, nobody even knows how to write with a pen anymore so there really is no going back.

The truth is though, technology is great – when it works. The problem is that a lot of the time, it doesn't. Computers crash more often than stock car racers - automated telephone systems behave like robots with a grudge and mobile phones keep us so connected that we have to regularly 'accidentally' lose them in order to get a minute's peace.

So, here are some guidelines as to how to deal with some typical techno-terror scenarios:

Your computer freezes – Send it on a package holiday to Malibu where it can thaw out and maybe go on a Jet Ski Ride or two.

Your solar powered calculator won't work because it's cloudy – Learn to add up or move abroad.

You Have No Internet Access – You'll just have to check Facebook on your mate's PC.

Your Mobile Phone Dies – Hold a memorial and then ask some boffins to see if they can invent a revolutionary telecommunications network that's a lot less complicated; one that uses the simple physics of sound waves vibrating from one handset, down a series of lines to another handset; one that dispenses with the whole 'mobile' idea and just refers to the devices as telephones.

Your Electronic Slideshow Won't Work – Bit of a radical suggestion but you might have to try and use that thing between your nose and your chin to communicate your ideas.

The Printer Refuses to Print – These devices have a mind of their own and it is an evil one. If you really need to print something and it won't print, you might have to consider a career change as this is likely to be less stressful than attempting to persuade the printer to change its mind.

The Photocopier is Out of Order – Call the repair guy and whilst you're waiting for him to come, make manual copies of the advertisement for the PS3 you're trying to sell.

The Coffee Machine is Out Of Order – This, of course, is a real crisis and no amount of expense or expertise should be spared to fix this problem. This can have a real effect on the profitability of the company as work cannot re-commence until this vital supply line is back on line.

'The supreme quality for leadership is unquestionably integrity. Without it, no real success is possible, no matter whether it is on a section gang, a football field, in an army, or in an office.'

Dwight D. Eisenhower

'The great thing about 'The Office' and it being single-camera and the documentary style is that it's mostly a comedy, but 10 percent of it is, we get to show the existential angst that exists in the American workplace.'

Rainn Wilson

'Our business is infested with idiots who try to impress by using pretentious jargon.'
David Ogilvy

Jargon Buster!

Yes, as if remembering which way to put your paper in the fax machine to ensure you're not sending 200 blank pages to the Brazil office (again) wasn't enough, you also have office jargon to contend with...

'Think Outside the Box'

...What?? Only hamsters on the journey home from the pet shop do their thinking inside a box! (How cute is it when they stick their little, pink noses out of the air holes by the way?!)

And what about Blue Sky Thinking...

"Sometimes, it's good to get a different perspective."

So, in a bid to prepare you - here are some of the finest pieces of pretentious piffle paffle you'll most probably encounter:

'Full Service', 'Robust', 'Boil The Ocean',
'Take Offline', 'Learnings', 'Reach Out',
'Hard Stop', 'Best Practices', 'Giving 110%,'
'Price Point', 'Leverage',
'Take It To The Next Level', '
Out of Pocket', 'Peel the Onion',
'Core Competency', 'Buy-In', 'Drinking the Kool Aid',
'Move the Needle', 'Tiger Team', 'Open the Kimono',
'Bleeding Edge', 'Burning Platform', 'Swim Lane', 'Lots of
Moving Parts', 'Corporate Values', 'Make Hay', 'Empower',
'Scalable', 'Ecosystem', 'Vertical'.

So what do you do?

'Aim for brevity while avoiding jargon.'

Edsger Dijkstra

Well, talking to BBC News Online *(http://news.bbc.co.uk/1/ hi/business/3014702.stm)*, John Lister of the Plain English Campaign states that jargon is *'...often used to hide the fact that you have got nothing to say,'* and believes its use has cost businesses millions of pounds (oops, somebody really *'pushed the envelope'* on that one *(towards the shredder – an envelope stuffed with millions of pounds!)*.

Lister states that it leads to people keeping schtum in meetings because they're not down with the downright dodgy lingo being batted around and end up *'timing out'*, trying to work out what the heck everyone's saying!

So the point is – avoid jargon like the plague. And if somebody says this to you:

'The benefit of having dedicated subject matter experts who are able to evangelise the attributes and business imperatives of their products is starting to bear fruit.'
(Marconi reorganisation announcement)

Tell them to go and upwardly implement a strategy for pragmatic self-resourcing in the robust realm of personal gratification!

'By working faithfully eight hours a day you may eventually get to be boss and work twelve hours a day.'

Robert Frost

'I have no ambition to govern men; it is a painful and thankless office.'

Thomas Jefferson

The Big Boss

Your decision whether or not to stay with the company
and climb your way to the top might well depend on
what you witness of your esteemed leader during your
time on the lower rungs.

Now, there are many, many bosses who are contrary
to what we are about to describe but it would seem
that there's something about being the boss that can, on
occasions, have an effect on the old grey matter. Whether
it's from eating too much caviar, spending too much time
in exclusive saunas or from repeatedly hitting your
head against a brick wall in sheer frustration – the boss's
brain cells appear to be at severe risk.

We don't have cure for this enigmatic ailment of the
upper echelons, but it is worth bringing to your attention
so you can bear it in mind when dealing with the boss.
However, whilst we may have some sympathy for the
stresses a boss might be under and the subsequent
effects, there are some things that a boss should never
say to you – and here some examples:

You're mowing my lawn this weekend, Anderson. Clothes are optional.

Warm your hands – I need you to check something.

Earlier today, my dog ate my wedding ring and, by the way he is circling, it may be about to re-appear. Be a dear, won't you?

This is a family business and I consult my father on everything. That reminds me, have you paid the Medium's invoice yet?

I'm a risk taker and always have been. By the way – it's no biggie if this month's payroll is temporarily in the hands of Mr. Luckie, my bookie, is it?

There are two types of people in this world. Me and Nobodies.

If a man comes in today claiming to have won this company in a card game, tell him to go to hell and that he's delusional, - but buy me a sombrero and book me on a flight to Mexico, this afternoon.

I've told you before – never enter my office when an item of clothing is wrapped around the door handle!

Please bring me a list of all the single men who are desperate to progress, oh, - and some whipped cream.

I have literally got my knickers in a twist. Bring some scissors and steady your hand!

I think one of our competitors may have booby trapped my car in a bid to see me off. Jump in and start it up, will you?

I've been the head of finance for 40 years and I still think FTSE is something you do under a table.

Who the hell is Dow Jones and why is he always down?

I want to see the latest figures - hand these bathing suits out to the staff.

This business is on the up! Sorry, I mean on its uppers!

No one man can make the decisions I have to make, alone. Hence the call girls.

I've put you forward as the company mascot. It saves us the expense of making somebody else look like a clown.

Don't worry - I've had some very good forecasts about the company for the fourth quarter.
She also said that a stranger would enter my life and the movement of Saturn could be a sign of good health!

How is it, Nicola, that I'm the boss but you're the one who's constantly giving me a raise, wink, wink?

What do you mean you're calling a mutiny because of a lack of education? Please, tell me what you mean – I don't know what a mutiny is!

I have hidden your pay packet somewhere about my person.

After my operation, toileting has become a little difficult and you've always said you're prepared to get your hands dirty...

Did my father ever love me? I never found out who he was.

Do these pants look better with, or without a crotch?

Tell me – what can you smell on my fingers?

If my wife calls, tell her I'm with my mistress, and if my mistress calls, tell her I'm with my wife.

BOSS: Do me a favour and fire that snivelling, brown-noser Smith, will you? Just tell him it's cut backs or something.

EMPLOYEE: I'm Smith, Sir and it's been an honour working with you!

OK. So does my bum look big now, without the pants on.

Tell your mother to iron my underwear before returning it to me next time, will you, Johnson?

I know you father's very proud of you – his pillow talk is really soppy.

Fetch me my horse.

Ninety years ago, we built this company on trust. But people are much more gullible these days so get out there and sell this rubbish!

Do you know, sometimes, when I look at you Jacobs, I'm reminded of my own son. His mother and I tried our best but what can you do?

If you really think that dressing like Rihannah is inappropriate then help me unchain my crotch!

"I've come to relieve you"

"I hope you've locked the door"

'When people say to me: would you rather be thought of as a funny man or a great boss? My answer's always the same, to me, they're not mutually exclusive.'

David Brent, 'The Office'

'What happens to a company if you take the boss away. I will answer your question with a question. It's like what happens to a chicken, when you take its head away. It dies. Unless you find a new head. I need to see which one of these people have the skills to be, a chicken head.'

Michael Scott, 'The Office' (USA)

'I have yet to find the man, however exalted his station, who did not do better work and put forth greater effort under a spirit of approval than under a spirit of criticism.'

Charles Schwab

'If you don't understand that you work for your mislabelled 'subordinates,' then you know nothing of leadership. You know only tyranny.'

Dee Hock

> *'Science may never come up with a better office communication system than the coffee break.'*
> **Earl Wilson**

Water Cooler Moments

It's a bit of a cheesy expression that's probably made its way into mainstream language from a rubbish rom-com but water cooler moments really do occur in offices and not everyone is well equipped to deal with them.

The first thing to point out is that they don't all occur at the water cooler. Basically, they're moments that occur in a normally quietish part of the office where people are doing something that isn't work related and therefore have an opportunity to chat.

So it could be at the water cooler, the vending and coffee machines or in the break room. Wherever they occur though, they can be a crucial component in the myriad of social systems and dynamics at work in the office community.

For example, the water cooler might be the place where a group of female colleagues all 'happen' to congregate at the same time. This coincidence allows them to rapidly exchange gossip whilst taking token sips from their freshly sourced water.

However, there is more to this than meets the eye. Amidst the raging and quite often unfathomable battle for gossip in the office, these group gossip moments are sometimes the subject of espionage. Outsiders to the group, who are normally members of a rival gossip group, will slowly walk by in a bid to overhear what's being said but once identified, the water cooler group will adopt a defence consisting mainly of a charm offensive. This means they will be overly nice and overly loud with their greetings to the spy which in turn, alerts members of other gossip groups in the area that they have successfully booed away a spook.

This is a very potent display of strength and an integral component in the group's bid for gossip dominance. This may well seem sexist but any man reading this will be thinking, 'Oh, yeah, I've noticed those girl gatherings – I normally just see them as a chance to perve!' and any woman reading will, even if she won't admit it, recognise the battle tactics.

'On **'The Office'** so much of the show is about disguising your true feelings and your romantic feelings because it was a mock documentary.'

Mindy Kaling

Of course – outside of the Gossip Gang Warfare, there is a much more appealing, romantic and, on occasions, a simply heart breaking type of water cooler moment. This is when a pair of colleagues who fancy each other, but are both too shy to seek conversation, bump into each other at the water cooler. If you're spectating from afar, you can usually identify this kind of scenario by judging how quickly the pairs' faces go from nought to red. These exchanges will often start by each person offering to let the other person fill their glass first but most men, no matter how shy, will insist that the woman goes first. Then, as the woman tries to hide the shake in her hand whilst she hovers her glass under the water cooler, there is an awkward pause.

This may only last a few seconds in reality but to the protagonists in this little play, it lasts a lifetime. And this pause is, of course, created by each person desperately trying to find something to say. Their first thought is to try and say something funny – especially if you're a man. Every female magazine/episode of Sex and the City seems to suggest that if a man can make a woman laugh – he's half way there (and yes, men do read and watch these things to try and learn a few things!).

Anyway, we all know that jokes are at their most elusive when we need them the most so that idea is quickly scrapped. They each now turn to the notion of commenting on something that mutually affects both people. The weather is the easy option but is dismissed due to its downright dullness and banality.

So, as the woman steps to the side, glass now full, the man has to step forward and he suddenly realises that as the woman has got what she came for (water), his time is running out. So, whilst filling up his sports bottle through the small nozzle, he turns to the girl and is about to say something when, with an excited whimper, the woman says, 'I'm getting wet!'

'Really?' The man says with a shocked and embarrassed smile.

'I mean, you're squirting it all over me!'

The boy, confused and embarrassed, looks down at his crotch before the girl jumps back and says, 'The water! You've got your nozzle too close to hole ... I mean – Oh, I've got to go!'

And with that, the one chance fate gave these two to start a beautiful journey into the world of romance together is well and truly dampened by a water – not so cool – moment. Tragic.

So, if you're one of these shy water slurpers – it can pay to have some ready-made conversation starters in the bank.

Some examples might be:

It's thirsty work this working for a living!

I'm afraid they've run out of tonic but there appears to be a barrel of gin with a tap on it if you're interested?

How's things over at your wing of the prison, I mean, side of the office?

Some people also say that you always tease the ones you like so a little gentle mickey taking might just do the trick:

Haven't I seen you before? Oh, that's it – Crimewatch.

Erm, I'm not sure if people from your side of the office are allowed to use this water cooler – this is for the cool side only.

I'm afraid this time's reserved for the talented people. Don't worry though, I'll say that you're with me!

However, there is definitely a fine line between gentle teasing and outright offensiveness – so you have to tread carefully with this tactic.

The 'Wrap'

The deadlines have been met, the job is done, the paperwork is filed and the system is updated. The customer is happy and even the boss is smiling because....

...the project's 'wrapped'.

This book is what we are talking about. We've just about come to the end of it. It only needs spell checking, formatting and editing and then we can go to the pub.

There are lot's of 'office stuff' that we haven't covered; wages, dress code, customers, dress-down Friday, afterwork drinking, to name but a few, but these and other subjects will be dealt with in...

"SURVIVE IN THE OFFICE WITH A SENSE OF HUMOUR – 2."

'I always arrive late at the office, but I make up for it by leaving early.'

Charles Lamb

Clocking Off...

Yes, it's everyone's favourite part of the working day – home time. We hope you've enjoyed our little guide to surviving life in an office. If you've taken in all of our advice and applied it at the office then, if we know our guides well enough, you're either currently being considered for the position of Chief Executive,

or reading this final sentiment whilst awaiting your appointment at the Job Centre.

Either way, it has been a pleasure working with you. Please hand your pass in at reception, empty the stationery you're hoarding in your pants (take care when removing the stapler) and be on your way. Feel free to take one last look at the place as you're leaving and give us a nice wave or, if you deem it to be a more accurate reflection of your feelings towards us, give us two fingers. Whichever you choose, we will humour you with a wave and with a pinch of sincerity – we'll wish you all the very best in your career!

P.S. The answer to our earlier teaser is Hull City ;-)